# Poems

Author:

Justin D. Mayberry

Editor:

Melissa Hines

Copyright © 2017 Justin D. Mayberry

All rights reserved.

ISBN:
**978-1544783116**

# DEDICATION

This is the first book I wrote since the passing of my dad.
I would like to dedicate this book to him.
R.I.P. Jerry Mayberry 2-8-15

## CONTENTS

1 **The Beat**

2 Love No More

3 *The End*

4 Volunteer

5 LOVE

6 Life

7 MOTHER

8 Winter

9 Spring

10 Summer

11 Fall

## CONTENTS CONTINUED

12  Grandmother's hands

13  Rain

14  Snow

15  How a kiss feel

16

17  Being a teenager

18  Marriage

19  You are my sunshine

## The Beat

THE NIGHTS ARE LONG
THE NIGHTS ARE COLD
WE WALK THE BEAT WITH OUR HEADS HELD HIGH.
EVERYONE IS SLEEPING NICE AND WARM IN THEIR HOMES AS WE WALK THE BEAT.
YOU HEAR OUT FOOTSTEPS ON THE SIDEWALKS THAT YOU WALK EVERY DAY.
YOU PAY US KNOW MIND UNTIL WE STOP YOU.
YOU OFTEN GET MAD AND HATE US.
BUT ALWAYS KNOW WE ARE WALKING THE BEAT TO PROTECT YOU AND YOUR PROPERTY.
UNTIL THE END OF OUR WATCH WE ARE HERE TO PROTECT.
SO WHEN YOU SEE THE HEARSE OF THE ONE THAT WALKED THOSE BEATS.
PLEASE STOP AND SHOW YOUR RESPECT
AS THE ONE THAT WALKED YOUR BEAT IS WALKING ANOTHER BEAT IN THE NEXT LIFE.

## Love No More

PAIN IS NO GAIN
PAIN HURTS LIKE HELL
WHEN I HAD TO LET YOU GO MY
HEART FILLED WITH PAIN.
I GAVE AND YOU GAVE BUT I
COULDN'T GIVE ANYMORE.
YOU CHOSE TO TOKE INSTEAD OF
LOVE
NOW WE MUST DEPART AND NOT
FEEL ANY LOVE.
FOR I HOPE YOU CAN CHANGE SO
ONCE MORE YOU CAN FEEL THE
LOVE THAT WE SHARED.

## The End

Days go on like they never end
We laugh and love until the end
We don't think life will ever end
But one day life does end
So show the one you love
The care and respect they deserve,
Because one day their life will end.

## Volunteer

We work day and night on call twenty-four seven.
We hear the beeps go off night and day.
We sometimes complain about never getting any sleep.
But deep inside we know we can't miss a call.
For we all like to make sure everyone is safe.
We scream down the roads trying to get there.
For someone is in need of help.
We don't do it for thank you, because it is a thanks job.
So when you see us coming down the road screaming.
Please move over so we can help the ones in need.
If you come across one
Please tell them thank you
Because one day you may need them.

## LOVE

Love is never ending.
We all get our hearts broke.
We all try to forget when it was broke.
Love makes us who we are.
Why don't people cherish the love?
For I don't know the reason people don't love.
We are taught as a child to love everything and everyone the same.
So why can't we move on past our difference.
And love

## Life

Life is hard
Life is tough
Life gives you mountains to climb
We have each other to help with these mountains in life.
You can give and give, and never receive.
Times get hard and times get great.
Sometimes you have to move on to see
That some things in life are better apart.

## MOTHER

She held you when you were first born
She held you when your heart was broke.
She laughed when you act silly
She cried sad tears when you left to go to college
She cried happy tears when you got married
She was the first one to hold your child
She will always be there for you even when you don't
think she will
So honor your mother ever day
Because one day she will not be here

## Winter

Time for all to rest
Time for the snow to fall
Time for children to make snow angels
The trees have no leaves
The cold nights so you can cuddle your love one
The long nights with the fire place and hot chocolate
Time to enjoy the slower paste
Before too long the weather will change, the snow will be gone and the children are out playing.
So enjoy this time with the love ones why can.
Spring will be here soon.

Justin D. Mayberry

## Spring

SPRING IS HERE
SPRING IS HERE
TIME FOR ALL TO START TO BLOOM
SCHOOL IS OUT
CHILDREN OUT PLAYING
HOUSES GETTING SPRING CLEANING
YARD SALE SIGN ARE OUT
TIME TO ENJOY THE SPRING WEATHER
SO GET OFF YOUR COUCH AND ENJOY
THE SPRING WEATHER.

## Summer

Time for school to be out
The sun is out in full swing
The heat is hot enough to cook an egg
The water is nice for a midnight swim
Time for friends and family get together
Time for the girls to wear the binkies and the guys to go shirtless
Time for the vacations for s life time
So don't let this summer go to waste
Have fun and enjoy the summer air

Justin D. Mayberry

## Fall

Time for leaves to fall
Time for the leaves to turn orange
Time for all the nightly gooles to come out and play
Time for the squirrels to gather their nuts
Time for us to get ready for the cold winter
Time for us to start a fire
Time for us to watch the cold nights to come

## Grandmother's hands

Her hands are so soft
Her love is so soft
She holds you when you are down
She rubs you when you're sick
She makes those homemade biscuits
She holds her grandchildren with care
She has done so much with those hands
For one day those hands will be gone
So cherish your grandmother's hands before they are gone and not so soft.

Justin D. Mayberry

# Rain

It comes down sometimes slow
It comes down sometimes fast
It comes down sometimes when the sun is out.
If you think about it rain is a lot like life
We cry when our life is torn by death and it seems nothing will go back to normal
We cry when children are born and seeing them grow up so fast.
We even cry when are rejoicing with the one you are marrying.
So next time it rains just think about how life is like rain.

## Snow

It is pure like a newborn baby
It falls so gracefully down to earth
Like an fallen angel
Children play in it
Adults become children again
It is a magical thing to see
So while it is here let's have fun no school no work let's play in the beautiful snow

### How a kiss feel

When you kiss the one you love it is like magic

The spark between the two there is no other feeling

Time stands still for what feels like forever

Holding and kissing the one you love

No matter how your day is going

The kiss from the one you truly love makes the day feel like magic every time

## Being a teenager

It is your adolescent years

Time to grow hair and get pimples

Time to make you parents worry

Time for you to think you know everything

Time to get your license

Time to get your first car

Time for graduation

Time for college

Don't let these years past by without out a good party

Before you know you will not be a teenager anymore so have fun while you can and live while you're young

Justin D. Mayberry

## Marriage

It's a time or joy
Time for rejoicing with the one you love
Time to dress in your best to impress
Time to give your heart away until one of you die
Time to grow old together making memories along the way
Times will be tough but just Remember that day you said I do.

## You are my sunshine

YOU ARE MY SUNSHINE.
YOU ARE MY HEART BEAT.
EVERY TIME I SEE YOU OR HOLD YOU
I AM AT PEACE.
YOU MAKE ME FEEL LIKE NO OTHER HAS BEFORE.
I WANT TO SHOW YOU THE WORLD.
THANKS FOR BEEN THE BEST.
YOU ARE MY SOUL MATE FOR LIFE.
YOUR LOVE IS LIKE THE AIR I BREATHE.
YOUR LOVE IS STRAIGHT AND CRISP.
YOUR LOVE MAKES ME FEEL SO MANY BUTTERFLIES.
YOUR LOVE MAKES ME WANT TO BE A BETTER LOVER FOR YOU.
EVERY TIME YOU TOUCH ME I FEEL YOUR ENERGY PASS THROUGH ME.
THANKS FOR BEING MINE AND GIVING ME LIFE, WITHOUT YOU LIFE WOULDN'T MEAN ANYTHING.

Justin D. Mayberry

Made in the USA
Columbia, SC
13 March 2022